An Ordinary Dog

GREGORY WOODS was born in Egypt and brought up in Ghana. He has two doctorates from the University of East Anglia (1983 and 2006). He began his teaching career at the University of Salerno, but is now Professor of Gay and Lesbian Studies at Nottingham Trent University. In addition to his poetry collections, all published by Carcanet, he is the author of a number of critical books, including *Articulate Flesh: Male Homo-eroticism and Modern Poetry* (1987) and *A History of Gay Literature: The Male Tradition* (1998), both from Yale University Press. He is an artistic assessor for Arts Council England and a Fellow of the English Association.

Also by Gregory Woods from Carcanet Press

We Have the Melon
May I Say Nothing
The District Commissioner's Dreams
Quidnunc

GREGORY WOODS

An Ordinary Dog

CARCANET

Acknowledgements

Earlier versions of these poems appeared in the journals *Ganymede*, *Gay and Lesbian Review*, *PN Review*, *Poetry Salzburg Review*, *Polari Journal* and *Staple*, as well as in the following anthologies: Amie M. Evans and Trebor Healey (eds.), *Queer and Catholic* (New York: Routledge, 2008), Jo Harding and Theresa Robson (eds.), *Slip Through the Silence: Facing Adversity with Verse* (Clitheroe: Clitheroe Books, 2008), *Kapow: New Writing with Impact* (Nottingham: Launderette, 2009), Gregory A. Kompes (ed.), *The Queer Collection* (Las Vegas: Fabulist Flash, 2007), *Reflections: A Collection of Poetry for the Waiting Room* (Derby: Reflections, 2007). 'Echo's Echoes' was first publshed on Twitter. I was awarded a second Hawthornden Fellowship in 2008.

First published in Great Britain in 2011 by

Carcanet Press Limited
Alliance House
Cross Street
Manchester M2 7AQ

ISBN 978 1 84777 078 3

The publisher acknowledges financial assistance from Arts Council England

Typeset by XL Publishing Services, Tiverton
Printed and bound in England by SRP Ltd, Exeter

Contents

Three

Four

One

Invocation

Come, hungry Muses, sink your fangs
into the rancid meat of things.
Give us another of those songs
that fizz the spittle on your tongues.

Descend on us in raucous gangs,
tattooed and sporting nipple rings.
Evacuate those tarry lungs
and goad us with your humour's prongs.

Conciliate your hunger pangs
with scraps of life, the random slings
and arrows felt by human throngs.

Foregather where the tyrant hangs,
and harry anyone who brings
to human rights inhuman wrongs.

Figure of Enchantment

She wears red feathers
but white ones on feast days
and on her birthday scales.
Her fingers have claws
and black talons for shoplifting.
When she swims she grows fins
and on the verge of drowning gills.
In her rump she hides a sting
for any man who crosses her,
but the stinging tastes of honey
just before it hurts.
The feathers she wears
are as red as her hair
and when anybody plucks them
she shrieks as if winning a prize.
Her annual ovulations
bring the kids out on the streets,
maidens waving bunches of mimosa
and square-bashing boys
with badges and berets.
By night she hides from headlights
as if running from the law.
When it snows she weeps for all mankind
(a colander) incontinently, out of earshot.
Those who fall in love with her
fall out again with broken hearts
and grazed extremities.
Nobody comes close.

Objective Disorder

Propriety once segregated us from girls,
and passion followed suit. No laws or papal bulls
applied to adolescent guile within these walls.
For all that we were rendered regular by bells,
each body's pulse subordinated to the school's,
mortality's unsentimental chisel gnarls
a boy's credulity, and scepticism kills
his faith. The gods he worships then are human pals,
imperfect but more beautiful than bloodless souls.
Beneath a plaster Virgin's blindness, like a doll's,
a pair of us replace cold prayer with spattered vowels
of inarticulate delight. Each of us feels
himself, unlike the sheets our ecstasy defiles,
unspoilt by the division of our bodies' spoils.

Age of Gold

Philosophy relied on words for its account
of love, but boys did well enough with groan and grunt.
Theirs was a class of flesh so laudable, by dint

of youth, that nothing but its semen should anoint.
Once they had passed beyond the point of do and don't,
they were held back by nothing worse than can and can't.

Pragmatic passion knew no more severe restraint
than the available, the possible – and want.
Besides, the cornucopia was never spent.

Landscape/Portrait

Devise a composition, taking in
the landscape, either as it stands or else
adjusting it to suit a preconceived
idea of how it might have looked if you

could see it from a higher vantage point,
or if a certain crag or tree were to
be shifted left or right, and when you point
your predatory telescope at it,

like some conquistador confronted by
the confirmation of a hunch that brought
him to the distant beach on which he must
find gold or die for having cost the crown

more than it takes to raise an army to
suppress a rebel province – take your time;
enjoy the passive scene as much as it
appears to be enjoying being seen.

Like a boy's body waiting to be kissed,
impatient for the tickle of the lips
or self-indulgent slaver of the tongue,
the sweep of him exposed across the broad

horizon of an unmade bed and crudely
sun-lit underneath the open window,
but hoarding shadow and a secret heat
in inaccessible but dreamt-of parts

unmapped by naked eye, still less explored
by stealth of touch, intoxicated breath,
the sweep of the eyelash or sputter of seed –
the landscape has its own apartness, chines

of shaded equilibrium where who
can tell what villainous conspiracies
have found their breeding ground, what animals
survive extinction unpoliced by law

of nature or decree of humankind,
and who knows who arrive in pairs to flee
the light and seek a new intensity
of heat within each other's arms and mouths.

The boy the landscape calls to mind believes
in his imagination and delights
the one complacent hand with which he tests
its truth to nature, idly fingering

the surfaces the look of him consists of,
comparing like with like, left side with right,
before exploring for a texture so
unsimilar as to appear the mark

of an unlikely cross with hairier
or hotter-blooded beasts, at intervals
sniffing his fingers for a sharper sense
if not of who he is of what he might

become, reluctant to commit himself
to depth till certain of its consequence,
inflicting with a pinch or gentle prod
enough of an impression to impress

upon himself a sense of life and risk,
with the flat of his hand assessing how
a pair of bodies might conceivably
become the tangle of a single fate.

The Best Medicine

This is me, laughing. And this one is my
brother and me on the boat, both laughing.
We're sending ripples out across the pond.
In this one we are trying not to laugh,
but laughing all the same. When my sister

joins us for this sequence in the garden,
she has got hiccups from laughing too much
and all three of us have tears in our eyes.
Even my father is shaking the camera,
pretending not to be amused at all.

There was the time in the minster – this is
the one – when someone came across to us
to ask us why we were laughing so much.
We hadn't stopped since we came in the door.
We are laughing, said my mother, because

(and here I pick up my father's camera
to capture, as they say, the occasion)
because, she says, our lives are amusing.
And she begins to laugh, her laughter as
infectious as any we've ever heard.

Even when fighting we couldn't help but
laugh at the pain we were inflicting or
suffering, laughable with its bruises
and tears. My brother laughed as he hit me
and I doubled up, laughing for dear breath.

Then what do you think we did when the dog,
with that usual laughing look on his face,
ran out into the road regardless of
the furniture van, squealing with its brakes?
What else could we have done – what else but laugh?

There must have been something in the water
for ten or fifteen years, something funny
in the water while we were growing up,
constantly triggering our reflexes,
leaving us helpless with mirth. Our shoulders

shook whenever silence was asked of us:
for one would always set the others off.
Our voices rang out in wave after wave,
feeding each other's laughter with laughter,
heartily laughing at nothing at all.

Faith Figure

A statue could have been more beautiful –
but not by much.
When he stands on this slab
and holds still
it proves impossible to pass him by.
They have to stop, to look.
A bronze could not have been harder,
colder to the touch,
more fearful in its unblinking glare
or more artful.
He mesmerises all of them
and holds them all to ransom.
Even during working hours
small crowds look up to him.
Do they imagine he needs to feel loved?
Could he possibly be lonely?
In the creases where his eyebrows meet
bewilderment can be inferred,
but only if the rigour of
his gaze and jaw line are ignored.
Seen from behind, he has wings
folded between his shoulder blades
but no one ever sees him fly.
Keeping up with his mere walking pace
is difficult enough.
With nothing more intelligent to do
than follow in his wake,
a certain sort of person
leaves decisions up to him.
Where to go. When to sleep.
How soon the comet will return.

Scenes from Stendhal

1   A very handsome youth,
he spent his life in the woods
with a hammer in one hand.

2   I shall willingly go to Naples
to read theology:
it is a labyrinthine discipline.

3   Everything is simple to his eyes,
for he sees everything from above.
How to conquer such a foe?

4   Every augury is breaking the rules
and running the risk of pre-empting events.
The upshot? Collapse of the whole system,
like a pyramid of cards or children's bricks.

5   I predict unpredictable seasons.
In fifty years, perhaps, the world
will have no further use for wasters.

6   The law is clear, he said.
As anyone can see,
your brother did not hurt himself
(as he claims)
falling off a ladder with an open penknife in his hand.

7   He cut this expression from the letter
with his blade
and destroyed it there and then.

8   Can it be, he went on, that what we call love
is yet another illusion? I'm as sure I'm in love
as I'm hungry at six in the evening. Can it be,
and how can it be, that out of such an appetite
those perjurers contrived Othello's love, and Tancred's?
Or was I alone made differently from other men?
Was mine of all souls made to lack one passion?
How capricious of Fate to have done such a thing!

9   Fabrizio
had forgotten
he was sad.

10   It happened, when Fabrizio arrived there,
that the room called Passive Obedience
was occupied by a hundred rats
which scattered in all directions.

Scenes from Flaubert

1   When their master called them
they would all march back
by gardens threaded with little rills
and then along the boulevards
in the shade of the old walls.
Their footsteps echoed in the empty streets,
the gates opened
and they would climb the stairs feeling glum,
as if coming home from an orgy.

2   They used to leave open the door
between their bedrooms
and chat from bed to bed.

3   Having observed high society only
through the looking-glass of his own
fevered ambition, he pictured it
as a contraption that functioned with
mathematical exactitude.
In a series of linked reactions,
a dinner party, a meeting with
a man of high status and a pretty woman's smile
could have spectacular results.
The drawing rooms of Paris
were like machines that
when you feed them raw materials
repay you a hundred times over.

4   The entirety of his knowledge
came from two books: *The Crimes of Kings*
and *Secrets of the Vatican*.

5   The simplest folk song
     held more poetry
     than the whole output
     of all the nineteenth-century lyric poets
     put together. Balzac was overrated,
     Byron vanished without trace,
     Hugo knew nothing about drama,
     blah blah blah…

6   The bohemian was sitting at the table
     drawing silly faces
     and the lawyer was dozing on the sofa
     in muddy boots.

7   Frédéric stammered, struggling for words,
     but then held forth about twin souls:
     there was a power that could vanquish space
     and bring two people together,
     apprising them of their feelings for each other.

8   The sinking of a
     passenger steamer
     kept them amused for
     as long as a year.

9   Adamant that he would never enter that house again
     or have anything more to do with people like those,
     he did not understand society's limitless capacity
     for indifference. He fancied he'd offended them.

Transformed into a god whose body could redeem
the very sins it succoured, mortal and extreme,
he was enough to make a Carmelite blaspheme.

When he appeared, first drawing human shape from steam
among the lesser members of the rugby team,
we had to hide the evidence of our esteem.

Although of boys the manliest, and of the cream
the very cream, his modesty could make him seem
provisional, the barest notes towards a theme.

Determined not to leave the groves of academe
(as our headmaster called his punishing regime),
without a solid grasp of how he reigned supreme,

we each put into practice plots to mine his seam
and plumb his arse, a speleologist's wet dream.

La Vie en Rose

1

One foot bare, the other in a satin slipper
worn away to next to nothing, she has placed
her basket of roses on the red earth.

She is gazing at the boy's black plimsolls.
Her father holds her hand while talking to
the fat old man in the red leotard.

Everyone has been trying to teach her
balance and silence, but she keeps falling
and crying, falling and crying, always

doing the wrong thing. She comforts herself
by singing, and the other children stop
bullying her until she stops singing.

2

She's kneeling, sitting back on her haunches,
her knees so far apart the short blue skirt
is tight as a drum skin across her lap.

Pressing hard on each thigh, she raises her
closed eyes to the slate-grey heavens and howls.
Rehearsal? Performance? Reality?

Wherever she sings, a crowd sustains and
drains her. But to physic the solitude
she administers her own remedies,

abstracting herself with another shot
of morphine and a hypodermic boy...
Falling and crying, always the wrong thing.

Strokes

The pain of Sunday
afternoons. Life of
a mayfly, urgent

with ungainly grace,
coming to its end.
Boredom is waiting

for Purpose to come,
as ever. He's late.
A tall, pale skinhead

leaning on his car,
pretty as a saint.
He strokes his tummy

under the T-shirt,
confronting my stare.
He's called Johnny, his

friend calls him Johnny
from inside the shop.
For me he lifts the

shirt with the upstroke
and plants a finger
in the wet navel.

When I step into
the shop his friend stands
politely to one

side for me to pass,
easing the pain of
Sunday afternoons.

Action and Reaction

The dispossessed and hopeless brood
in bars where anarchy is brewed

until such time as they can't wait
to prove that they can pull their weight.

With banners, flags and solemn rites
they gather to demand their rights,

aware that dictum number one,
Rights Are Not Handed Out But Won,

is more than just a pious phrase
to be deployed when patience frays.

A demonstrator in the throes
of growth confirms himself and throws

a stone, as if a stone he threw
had any chance of getting through

from the redoubt where it was thrown
to hit the target on the throne.

He contemplates his fates with awe:
an unmarked grave at sundown or

for cigarettes and needles sell
his body in a prison cell.

Remote from times he never knew,
he thinks that what he does is new,

so slow to grant his elders their
involvement in his being there.

While indoors those who matter wine
and dine, outside the scroungers whine.

While each mouth sips expensive liquor,
each arse is waiting for its licker.

A scream and conversations lapse.
(Some spill their vino in their laps.)

All the assembled diners freeze
like figures on an Attic frieze.

The sound of distant gunfire pours
into the panic of their pause.

The stone flies from its angry source,
through glass, into a tasty sauce;

en route it breaks a stained glass pane,
which causes idle aesthetes pain.

A lawyer feels the chilly draught
around his neck and starts to draft

a decent public order law.
Deriving strength from ancient lore,

he plots revenge. He'd love to get his claws
into the culprits, clause by clause.

A programme of excuses bawled
by senators infirm and bald

and threats disguised as wisdom brayed
by asses dignified with braid

are broadcast on the air to rouse
the suburbs with their raucous rows.

They'd mobilise the army's might
to scratch an itch or squash a mite.

Unruly aspirations grate
against What Made the Nation Great —

but listen while the common herd,
who should be neither seen nor heard,

reveal the fundamental flaw
in not the carpet but the floor.

Envoi

To find the carcass of your son
uncovered by the risen sun,

to see him lying, shattered, bare,
is more than human life can bear.

A squaddie while the mother grieves
adjusts the buckles on his greaves.

Initiation

There came a moment when the boy was blessed
with manliness: *et homo factus est.*

We raised a glass to him as he undressed,
deliberately slowly, shirt then vest,

revealing first his belly, then his chest,
before the next and final step, the best:

a theory of man, made manifest.
It was a sight you couldn't not molest,

especially since he'd never been caressed
but by himself, by hand. We pounced, with zest,

and he began to weep – he'd never guessed
what fun mere fun could be! He deliquesced,

exuding, oozing, spurting, seeping – stressed
to be releasing all that he'd repressed.

Ah the Taste of a Stranger's Mouth!

I was reading a sentimental novel
    when the bus conductor prised
    my lips apart with his tongue
and spat down my gullet. He had been eating
    cherries, pips and all, as if
determined that at least one should take root in
    his appendix and put shoots
    out through his belly-button –
he could have sold the sweaty
blossom to bridesmaids. I drugged
myself on nicotine licked from between his teeth.

I was the only passenger on the upper
deck. Whenever we approached a bus stop he
rang the bell twice to tell the driver not to
stop. I was watching first-floor windows. I saw
    secretaries seeing me –
they tended to drop their pencils and notepads.
My novel had dropped into my lap, tent-like
    over my stiffening prick.

'Greg,' I gurgled when I first came up for air,
    offering him my hand to
shake. 'Otis,' he said, and he squeezed my reading
    matter till I squealed. So much
for small talk. I shoved my unused handshake hand
into the sweltering fork of his trousers.
I'd not had time to ask him if I was on
    the right bus, but time would tell.

We were nearing the end of the line. Catching
my breath, a trickle of Otis's spittle
        on my chin, I remembered
the punchline of a joke. Otis told me he
comes off duty late. Do I ever go to
        the Toaster? The what? 'It's a
        club, man, a dive!' He slipped me
        the card: line drawing of a
        toaster. Hot slices spinning in the
        air. 'From half eleven. See
        you there?' He wears pink Reeboks.

But I lied when I said Greg. It seemed like a
        good idea. I wanted to
be like the famous spy before he's famous.

The Picture with the Bear

Alma has swept her hair back from the brow
with her right hand and with the left index
finger is caressing the shaggy bear
between its eyes. She must be more frightened
than she looks! Yet the frankness of her gaze
into the lens is more suggestive of
a triumphant hunter with his carcass.
The beast itself, as represented by
that single jet-black eye, conveys as much
or as little as you might expect. Alma!

Are you soothing or irritating him?
While Alma fixes the photographer
with her usual sparkle and half a smile,
he her with the thrust of his obsession,
suppose an ursine plot were being hatched,
complete with roar to shake the window panes,
stinking of salmon, and a flash of fangs...
Alma's pale cheeks, her opalescent eyes!
For all I know, this very second's pop
and flash may have panicked the animal

and Alma, momentarily blinded,
may have made things worse with a piercing scream.
That voice has sung so many parlour songs,
and out of earshot earthier lyrics
of her own devising, expressions of
her more pressing concerns; yet what is left
for it now but a brief and futile cry
for help? The man behind the lens, of course,
committed to his sinister art, sees
only focal length and composition,

plunging though he is into those three eyes
as if hypnotising or hypnotised.
As for myself, I feel as if I could
address any remark to Alma or
ask her any question and she would half-
smilingly reply with something cryptic
or ambiguous, something for me to
misinterpret in my habitual way,
with undertones of promise or menace,
savoury nothings to remember her by.

Figure with No Past

He forgets. Some lobe
or ventricle has atrophied
and left him searching for a past
he has to reconstruct
from souvenirs and guesswork.
When he invents events
he claims to have remembered them –
a book of fables shelved as history.
But when he remembers
and his eyes fill with tears
it makes no sense to doubt him,
any more than Aesop
should be fingered as a fibber.
(This frog, this raven, this fox,
this ant, where's the evidence?
Show us the proof, this jackdaw,
this slavering but rational wolf.)
In the cool of the evening
he waxes nostalgic
and even leaves silences
for the things he's suppressed.
By the time it comes
to dreaming, his unconscious
harbours nothing but
the mechanism for the job:
axon synapse dendrite
dendrite synapse axon...
He sleeps as deeply as a submarine,
a cistern or a saint.

Figure of Achievement

He's in it for himself
but others sunbathe in
the splendour of his trophies.
Never satisfied,
he's always either poised for marks-set-go,
alertness throbbing in his ears,
or panting from his latest win.
Acolytes refresh his armpits with their tongues
and carry off his turds in pewter bowls.
He indulges all idolaters,
a smile, a wave, an unmeant compliment,
but suffers no agnostics,
let alone the few who openly
consider him the next worst thing to Baal.
Tiny phials of his sweat
have been smuggled in towels from the locker room
and the market in his jock-straps
remains bullish, as ever.
The crowds who cheer him
gather in the stadiums days in advance
and even pack the surrounding streets,
chanting his name, chanting his name,
herded behind barriers by mounted police.
Even in the smallest towns
subscription lists have been compiled
for the erection of statues.
The beds he sleeps in
are kept for posterity, unmade.
While anyone who touches him without permission
is taken to be flogged,
the few he touches of his own volition
become impossibly conceited.
Those who never dream of him
are sectioned for the public good.
You can never be too careful
when it comes to the Unconscious.

Messages

My love, I'm waiting for the phone to ring,
      For you to answer all
      The messages I left
Or for at least some other friend to bring
      Relief to my bereft
      Expectancy, a call
            Out of the blue
That I might for a moment hope was you.

I wonder where you are and what you're doing
      – As if I haven't guessed –
      As if the fact of knowing
Who else you're eating with or even screwing
      Could set my mind at rest.
      I've been too easy-going.
            I bet you're plastered,
Too drunk to care, you egocentric bastard.

I used to be your most naïve believer.
      It doesn't take a Freud
      To see I should evade
Interpreting my phone's inert receiver,
      But call me paranoid:
      You're either getting laid
            Or on your own
At home, not deigning to pick up the phone.

That's far more likely: loftily detached,
      You monitor your calls.
      Your answering machine,
Equipped with diplomatic skills unmatched
      By any go-between
      Indifferently stalls
            Both foe and friend
Alike. Do you not care whom you offend?

I languish here, entangled in the flex,
        Without a chaperone,
        Soft-fingering your number
As if caressing someone's flaccid sex
        To rouse it from its slumber.
        Perhaps it's not the phone
                But you who's dead.
Perhaps I need a ouija board instead.

Is there anybody there? One knock
        For yes, two knocks for no.
        Who would have thought we'd not
Outlast the rigor mortis of your cock,
        Our silence from a plot
        By Edgar Allan Poe?
                How I'd rejoice
Even to hear an insult in your voice!

My spicy fantasies of you have ceased
        To work. I may be lonely,
        But you're the bloody wanker.
If not for your neglect, I could at least
        Attempt a dash of rancour:
        You see, if you would only
                Communicate,
I might feel able to reciprocate.

Trees or Fly-Fishing

for John Greening

I suppose a Professor of Gay and Lesbian Studies has a professional obligation to write about these areas, but I'd have welcomed a few poems about trees or fly-fishing
John Greening, London Magazine

1 Trees

A boy has found a comfy place to perch
Among the branches of a silver birch,
A giant fledgling, ignorant of flight,
His *raison d'être* a growing appetite.

He's edging higher, coveting the breeze,
– When, whoops! young Zoltan snags his dungarees
Upon a wayward branch and down they come,

Exposing genitals and peachy bum
(The fleecy gold of the Hesperides)
In one fell swoop. Uncommon though the trees

That bear such appetising fruit as these
May be, a clement godhead might endow
Whole orchards with such ripeness on the bough.

2 Fly-Fishing

Casting their lines upon the sluggish flood
To stir if not its flow each other's blood,
Two boys are fishing at a river's edge,
Serene among the reeds and swaying sedge.

But one by accident then casts his fly
In the direction of his playmate's shorts,
Or by design, co-ordinating eye
And hand, and hooks the object of his thoughts.

Considerate and mercenary, he tries
To free his errant hook from Laszlo's flies
And manages to spring a big surprise –
Engorged, engaged, impertinent, improper!

He's never had a thing within his grasp,
Though like a chubby chub at its last gasp,
So full of life as this enormous chopper.

It leaps and slithers in young Zoltan's hand.
But who will, when his mortal span is spanned,
Believe those tales of landing such a whopper?

When You Go

Before the bar staff start collecting glasses
And calling time, as other men prepare
The night's diversion, making random passes;
Approach me with a smile, as if you know
No fear, ask me to share your taxi fare,
        And take me with you when you go.

If we should sit up, practically till dawn,
Discussing literature and world affairs,
Until the final phrase becomes a yawn
And tiredness staunches conversation's flow;
Embrace me, make your weary way upstairs,
        But take me with you when you go.

Before the night is over, having swapped
Positions, taking pleasure to extremes
Until completely beat, and having stopped
Performing, to and fro, our quid pro quo;
Make sure, as you withdraw into your dreams,
        You take me with you when you go.

Although we've tempered the initial thrill,
The future beckons and, against the odds,
It looks as if the two of us are still
Together, hungry for a bungalow.
So when you put your plans in place, for God's
        Sake take me with you when you go.

And even when our hopes run out of time,
And death is just a breath away, the bells
Already muffled and the pit of lime
Already dug, prepare a cheerio –
But count yours truly out of your farewells.
        Please, take me with you when you go.

Envoi

Call me a moron, claim I smell,
Or tell me my ideas repel.
I don't mind if you kick or clout me.
But if at any time you doubt me,
       Go to Hell –
       And go without me.

Scenes from Gautier

1   Whatever I'm waiting for,
    it's definitely nothing
    mundane or ordinary.

2   So many pathetic specimens
    for just one Antinous!

3   I think, my dear friend,
    that at this point I should insert
    a line of dots, since the rest
    of this conversation
    could hardly be represented but
    with a sequence of noises

    . . . .

4   The squire as beautiful as a woman,
    his page as beautiful as a girl.

5   'I am in love.'
    There's no pleasanter sentence
    to keep saying to yourself,
    tucked up in bed, head on a soft pillow,
    under a thick quilt,
    no more agreeable four-word sentence
    – except of course
    'I have some money.'

6   If you were covered
    from head to toe
    in the thickest of cloaks
    I would still recognise you
    by one of your fingers.

7   It's hard to speak of love
    to someone in the same clothes as yourself
    and wearing riding boots.

The Sweet Life

I hadn't even said his name to myself
for years until this afternoon, when I heard
        myself whisper it as I shopped
        for groceries, struggling to opt

for one brand rather than another, with no
interest in either. As if to summon him
        for help from some lobby of death,
        I cited him under my breath.

I used to talk to him whenever I could,
on the cold staircase that spiralled around the
        forever out-of-order lift,
        the folly of our fifties-quiffed

caretaker; or on a bench under the plane
trees in front of our building, where he used to
        sit and read when his younger brothers,
        driven to screaming by each other's

legitimate aspirations, drove him out
of the family home. Learning English, he
        initially treated our meetings,
        which hardly went further than greetings

and comments on the weather, as extensions
of his lessons, dutifully expanding
        his repertoire of adverbs, ready
        for paths down which he was unsteady,

trying out the odd cliché caught from a film
or unwittingly airing a redundant
        scrap of slang from an out-of-date
        text book. But he started to wait

for me even when the terrible brothers
were out playing football, and when we met it
        became less important to talk
        all the time. We'd go for a walk,

even lapsing into Italian or the
silence of friendship. I fell in love with him
in the streets, but left this unsaid
until he could hear it in bed.

In every boy's future there's the middle-aged
man his body will become in spite of him:
feeding his regrets, he'll fatten
and go to seed, the common pattern.

By now he must be married and have sons of
his own he'll scold when he catches a whiff of
tobacco on their breath. He no
longer knows the places to go,

for the city changes all the time and a
father has little time to explore it; but
I wonder if he ever follows
a boy into those scrubby hollows

where the railway line begs to differ from the
curve of the river and people dump their old
fridges, if he risks an attack
to grab an hour of boyhood back.

That was a spot I often used to go to,
after dark, before I met him, searching for
excitement or solace, but then
I never visited again.

When he first came back to my flat, we hurried,
giggling, past his place on the lower floor and
I pushed him into my dark hall.
We came to rest against the wall

of my bedroom, in such urgent need that we
hardly bothered searching for the door handle
but grappled with each other there,
ripping clothing aside to bare

something less tangible than flesh, more fleeting
in its way; and when I lowered him to the
            marble tiles he cried out in more
            than shock at the coldness of the floor.

When I'd made him coffee and sent him downstairs
to his parents' home he cheerily shook my
            hand as if I'd just been giving
            an English lesson, or living

in that place at that time routinely involved
feral spats of debauchery on the floor.
            Occasional meeting became
            regular, always with the same

intense beginnings and nonchalant endings,
even as our affection turned into love;
            and that thirsty summer was spent
            in each other's lives. When he went

off on his National Service and I came back
to England, I made the effort to pretend
            the past was past and nothing jerked
            it back into motion. It worked.

Instead, when I thought of that town I used to
conjure up my nights on the river bank, half
            crazy with appetite, cruising
            any shadow and confusing

trees for men, but somehow drunkenly finding
enough of what I was seeking to make it
            worth coming back, night after night,
            following dark outlines, despite

the risk, through darker spaces, almost blind, week
after week, man after man. With all that to
            remember, I'd forgotten how
            much that one boy meant. Until now.

Last Resorts

He spurns Apollos you'd have thought were certs:
this Jason to unworthy Argonauts

attracts a retinue of introverts
whose slightest willingness to please he thwarts

with condescension so severe it hurts –
as if a smirk could melt a lump of quartz –

and anything a nervous suitor blurts
he answers with uncompromising snorts.

The foolish supplicant forlornly flirts,
a speculator reconciled to noughts;

the wise (if such a man exists) averts
his eyes, preferring indirect reports.

Those sturdy nipples, like a pair of yurts
on barren steppes, or sullen Bronze Age forts!

We seek a weakness – though the thought subverts
our sense of him – the merest spots or warts

to reassure us human life reverts
to the reality a dream distorts.

His mere existence, in the flesh, perverts
the most reserved, conventional of sorts:

to breathe the sweat his energy exerts
in strenuous routines of manly sports,

we rummage in the laundry for his shirts.
The despotism of his feet extorts

our kisses, less deserving than the dirt's.
The sheer abundance of his Lycra shorts

exacts the tribute of our petty spurts,
and we are left with little but our thoughts,

those sorry spectres of our just deserts.
We make do with each other. Last resorts.

Figure of Opportunity

With arms as open as a wingspan
he suggests a welcome,
the overstated bonhomie
of the out-of-season Alpine innkeeper,
the hypocritical relief
of the prodigal father.
He spreads his fingers too,
an octave or a greedy grab,
and bares his phosphorescent teeth
against indifference.
When you get close enough
to be addressed, his mouth addresses you,
but what he says is hardly worth repeating:
the blandest of courtesies, a cradle of cliché
and one inconsequential joke.
Yet the truth is in there somewhere,
like garlic in a stew, unfindable
but on your breath and on your nerves all day.
He wants you to acknowledge him
as if he were a needy child
with some pathetic, ostentatious game
he's just invented.
A smile would be enough, a conversation more
than he could hope for.
But the wheeling shadow of the dying elm
and the hoarse, catarrhal hauling of the shingle by the tide
express a sense of urgency.
Seize anything if not the day:
the candlesticks, the bunch of keys, the poetry anthology…
Seize anything. But go, get going, go!

End of Eternity

A memory of heartburn
and the echo of a belch:

Ourobouros has swallowed
the last morsel of himself.

Two

Jerome

The picture of studious self-discipline,
he has abstracted himself from the scene and
allowed the landscape behind him to foreground
itself, importantly subordinating
himself to the passing universe of men.

Asceticism has a certain glamour
when you've taught yourself Hebrew for the Scriptures
and taken to resting your slippered feet on
the upholstered ribcage of a dormant lion.

For all that he seems unaware of the crowds
in posterity's gallery, I get the
impression this is how he wants to be seen.
At any rate, I don't credit him. Call me
trivial, but I can hear his stomach rumbling.

Into Battle

Across the river valley, eye to eye, we face
each other's fears, embodied in a blinding mass
of shields and breastplates, visors as expressionless
as saints, and bugles orchestrated to concuss
the very air with dread. Between us, like a sluice,
the glinting river waits to profit from our loss.
A day so fine should moderate the bellicose,
but orders drafted on a map must take their course.

There's nothing like a war to ready men for peace,
and nothing like their cowardice to make a farce
of tragedy. Not one of us could keep his voice
as firm as if delivering heroic verse,
once hurt, or beautify his body's sacrifice
with lips still masculine, still worthy of a kiss.

Newton at Woolsthorpe

Light penetrates a knot-hole in a shutter;
an apple falls. The universe's rules
apply no less to life's accustomed clutter
than to its galaxies and molecules,

and even the most unassuming shack
supplies in everyday domestic life
its own laboratory, the bric-à-brac
of physics: pitcher, mirror, candle, knife.

And yet it takes a Newton to deduce
that implication from the thing itself,
from any piece of junk its nobler use,
as yet unnoticed on the kitchen shelf:

as solipsistic as a pinchbeck ring
of alchemists, a knotted loop of string...

Interpreting Flaubert

Discretion and broad-mindedness: what more
could any traveller desire in his
interpreter, as much as in his common

Egyptian whore? From their disharmony
of broken wind and creaking bed-springs, I
devise a dialogue as if of equals.

Fastidious in the avoidance of
exact expressions, *les mots justes*, I strive,
since touching separates, to bring them closer,

and introduce refinements, editing
his native arrogance and her *ennui*,
in Arabic and French. I make myself

invisible but indispensable,
a go-between with no between to go.

Death of Rimbaud

Sometimes he calls me Djami. Tenderly,
remotely. I respond with what his tone
seems to require by way of comradeship.
A damp cloth on the forehead, soothing words,

respectful silence. Silence above all.
The hand I feel him squeeze may not be mine,
but my concern invites him to go on
elaborating his delirium.

A sister's love, boiled down to little but
the comfort of familiarity,
succeeds the intellect it came before.

The eyes he sees me with see someone else,
but love transcends identity, and life
is more than just another passing phase.

Jean Genet in Norwich

Adrift, becalmed but – knowing life – expectant,
directed by the smell of disinfectant
alone, he finds his way to Bishopgate,
where the cathedral dwarfs a brick and slate

ciborium. In darkness devotees
of a consuming faith sink to their knees
to celebrate with seasoned gravity
the rites of their refined depravity.

Asperged by sperm and leaky cisterns,
confessional, they minimise their distance,
each *mea culpa* a bouquet of faults.

He'll find the space beneath these mossy vaults
more homely than the home he never had –
as good a place as any. Or as bad.

Lenin on the Thérémin

Provided with sufficient power, one man
can conjure from a field of influence
a beauty forged in cauldrons of white heat.
The principle means more than the aesthetics.

This music is material, the ploughshare
of silence. I conduct an orchestra
of miners, engineers, technicians – all
the artisans of electricity.

Man is not passive in the face of Fate.
He shapes himself to fit his circumstances
and shapes his circumstances to himself.

When he needs melodies to work or march to,
his art is activated by a switch.
Such harmony the world has never known!

E.M. Forster at Rockingham

One may as well begin with the Commander.
Our host, who judges tardiness a crime,
applies the strategies of Alexander
to making sure a meal arrives on time.

When in repose he still emits a buzz
of bellicosity engaged by pique.
For lack of crew a wife will do – and does:
she soldiers on and turns the other cheek.

Outside, great yews like elephants close ranks
against a gale, but he with damn-and-blasts
and shooting-stick patrols the castle's flanks,
regardless. At each corner he *Avasts!*,

defensive yet aggressive, with aplomb,
to mark his birthright like a ginger tom.

His Philosopher's Voice

The rough, the smooth. A change of temperature. Intelligence
is all, but beauty might be worth a modest outlay. Love
would be enough, or failing love a condom full of seed.
Each style goes out of date before the thicker-skinned of us
have even noticed it was ever in; goes out of date
to be revived a decade later, out of date but in,
ironic, camp, supposedly sophisticated. Love
would be enough for anyone. The rough, the smooth; the dark,
the fair. The article, indefinite or genuine.
Deductive reasoning, dear boy (now wriggle out of those
impossibly indecent shorts), has elevated us
above the beastly beasts with no pornography or thumbs.
Deductive reasoning, they call it. That and vintage wine.
In that and that, and other things. In those we find ourselves,
the animal with thumbs to hold a glass of Châteauneuf.
Collateral, colostomy, solicitude and sweet
sagacity! By Jove, was that a whiff of Ganymede?

To the Authorities

Who is he waiting for, the hypostatic figure on
the pavement opposite the half-refurbished salad bar,
his fists embedded in deep pockets, collar up against
the rain or recognition, his defences up against
coincidence? Whose threats or promises have thrummed his pulse

to the absurd extent of bringing him to stand in this
forgettable location, cold, impatient, unaware
that promises can be forgotten, threats not acted on?
When will he cut his losses and go home, disgusted at
another wasted afternoon, another vain attempt?

How did it come to this? How did a boy so free of cares,
so breathless with expectancy, become this effigy
of unresolved miscalculation? When does such a man
remember how frivolity once energised his soul?

Preoccupations

The bathing cabins have already been dismantled.
The deckchair boys have put their winter woolies on
and gone back to the books they spent the summer months
neglecting (catering, computers, economics).
Nostalgic for the habits of display, they need

the hero-worship that their mirrors offer them.
Among the dunes, off-season visitors may find,
still held in place by marram grass, impressions of
those toppled statues of the gods, the hedonists
who spent the summer here, contriving perfect tans.

A man and dog are walking on the tide line. Dog
is hoping for a whiff of something tasty, man
for sex or anything to take his mind off sex –
a tidal wave or an amphibious assault.

Torso

It seems to help him think,
this absent-minded gesture
of presence on the part
of his unmindful hand.

He strokes himself in front
of each oblivious
old master, comforted
by physicality.

It also helps me think,
but not of course about
the art. Among these gods

and human victors he
alone partakes of what
you might call rapture.

In Derby Cathedral

Oasis from the traffic, this cool place
restores my balance, but its calm deceives
the senses, mimicking an open space,
its columns palm-trunks and its vaults their leaves.

Immune to Dogma's patronising pardons,
I think of Gide's immoralist among
the boys, inhaling in narcotic gardens
the scent of cannabis and donkey dung.

Man delves and spins, condemned to what pollutes
creation: human energy cremates
the trees of Eden, while this faith salutes

a nit-picker who differentiates
between forbidden and permitted fruits
as interchangeable as figs and dates.

On Derby Station

You hug me unrevealingly. Emotion
has ambushed me in its clandestine fashion
and left me mute. Yet wording your devotion,
you substitute a homily for passion:

Though at the risk of launching an obsession,
desire should be suppressed as a precaution;
for *Fire and brimstone, this shall be their portion* –
unless they wipe the slate clean at Confession.

Your parting words are like a boy's emission,
nocturnal and nonsensical, creation
distilled into an artless repetition:

untouched by candour or imagination,
the statement of a previous position,
I love you has become a mere quotation.

Drive-By

A casanova's dancing pump, the limo
performs a leisurely and polished shimmy,
a *paso doble* through the hills at dead
of night towards whatever act of god

or man its shooting script anticipated.
Since nothing happens but to be repeated,
prepare yourself to recognise your chances
from previously conjugated tenses.

Give life its due regard. The thread is lost
the moment you're distracted. When the bell
for bedtime rings in the asylum, lust

resolves itself and greed is spent like bile.
Yes, it's a drive-by life. It doesn't last
and nobody is held responsible.

Mothers of Sons

I am surprised that you are still silent. That can scarcely mean consent
Sigmund Freud, *The Question of Lay-Analysis* (1926)

The mothers were permitted
to address the tribunal
but nothing had been promised them
and nothing asked on their behalf.
They dressed for the occasion, some
as if to celebrate a prodigal's return
and some as if to bury him,
but all as if their lives
depended on appearances. (They did.)
A gavel was deployed
to pacify the hostile crowd.
What air conditioning could not achieve
a pair of cops with threatening expressions
managed: Arctic calm.
The time had come
for systematic accusation.

Mothers of unmanly men,
the evidence will show,
and lack of alibis corroborate,
not only that you loved your sons
but that you did so with
malevolent intent.
Mothers of milksops and sissies,
your bedtime stories kept your boys
awake with longing.
Mothers of weaklings and weeds,
you brought tears to their eyes
with the lemonjuice wince
of your emotional blackmail.
The best of them resisted the allure
of comfort – they were strong –
but for the rest the effort was in vain:
they couldn't whistle, throw a ball,

or impregnate a fertile womb.
Mothers of crybabies,
mothers of mother's boys,
mothers of sons,
your apricot kisses
exacted a terrible toll.

Settle to the task
of punishing yourselves
with what you thrive on. Guilt.

The mothers hang their heads
if not in shame in weariness
and dab their eyes with crumpled tissues
taken from their sleeves.
Permitted to address the court,
they shake their heads in silence.
How their failure to excuse themselves
incriminates them!
How their booming silence says it all!

Priorities

When we whose rootless salad days were coinciding
with the festivities of springtime and the budding
of oleanders reckless of our future fading
stepped out along the boulevards serenely nodding
our pretty heads and all but meaninglessly gadding

about with little more intention than the goading
of those who judged us and the diligent avoiding
of ever doing even by default their bidding
to save the morals they purported to be guarding
thereby exacerbating their splenetic brooding

our lives had no more urgent purpose than the feeding
of appetites from secret shames to extra pudding
and making pungent tatters of each other's bedding
allowing others to obsess about the wording.

Indictment

Any more questions? Has the time of fasting lapsed
already? And the season of
mellow mistiness? Does nobody round here
speak the dialect of my instructor?
If you had half a heart
and even a sliver of a brain,
wouldn't love have left us
with more than this numbness
and these nodding, weepy erections?

I'm running out of patience
with being patient, sitting on a hot rock
here at the side of the road,
where whole armies have passed, triumphant
or defeated, for centuries.
I buy balls of white cheese
from the herdsboys at dusk
and cup my hands in the gutter
for the sweetest of water.
For company I make do with ardent strangers.
Were I the seed-bed of a dynasty,
I couldn't be more forward-looking,
more open to change.

But I come from a family
of butchers and mechanics,
conditioned to practicality,
skinning and tuning this horrible world,
and thriving in the premises of weaker rivals.
Chewing their fingernails, my sons
and their sons will taste blood and oil.

What about you? Can you say the same?
Why all this talk about me?
Wasn't it you who told me
you were starting to doubt the existence
of horses, of feldspar, of echidna and of trust?
Didn't you see an assassin
in the eyes of every ardent stranger? Tell me,
where were you between two and five
on the morning of the fifteenth?

Three

Penmanship

And I looked at the pen and I said to myself, what the hell am I grabbing this for?
Arthur Miller, *Death of a Salesman* (1949)

I was having a conversation
in the nuthouse,
a conversation with two other nuts,
when something fast and blurry,
furry, scaly, feathery,
flew in the window.

Quick, said one of us
— not me —
let's trap it in the waste basket
and see if it's edible or sellable,
or, said another,
reducible to gunk or ash.

We bounced off the walls
in our comical attempts
to corner the stupid thing,
whatever it was,
and we bounced off each other
for the hell of it,
but didn't make a noise
in case the white-coats came to break it up.

This doo-dah landed on the lampshade
and it slid along the window sill.
We threw our cardigans at it
and little balls of bread,
but nothing worked.
It spread itself across the crucifix and,
squeaking, seemed to laugh.

That did it.
I took my writing implement,
the one without graphite or ink,
the one we're allowed,
the one that's seen me through these years,
the one the committee clamoured to see –

and I wrote with it, airily, wrote in the air,

I wrote about cages and springes and cats,
I wrote about bullets and arrows and stones,
I wrote about poisonous plants
and what you can do with ground glass,
I wrote with my right hand,
     I wrote with my left,
I crossed my bees and dotted my esses,
     adding ridiculous curlicues
     innocent of meaning,
writing with passionate involvement,
writing with detached objectivity,
writing for money and
     writing for love,
writing for the moment and
writing for eternity –

and even when I had written the final full stop,
and the other two loonies had settled me down,
     we looked for the thing,
     the thing that came in,
     the thing I'd forgotten,
and the thing I'd forgotten came in had gone out.

First Rites

The victim is bleeding, true to the role,
but nothing is said, nothing needs saying,
nothing but blood and what blood means to say.

The attendants are judicious: they cover the wound
with bibulous lint and a flutter of fingers,
hostile to paparazzi and blowflies alike.

The victim suppresses his hurt, all the more
to be respected for his stiff upper lip,
internalising all the blather of agony

for future use on unsuitable occasions:
a casual date, a taxi ride, the rearing of
a dimpled and beribboned daughter.

Memo: it is imperative that all should suffer,
if suffer they must, in silence, but each
in his own way, to his own illiterate script –

the personal touch. Let each one lament
a particular loss and secure it in his wallet
like a folded photograph. The men

exchange them in moments of tension,
caressing surfaces, pressing the gloss
for an impression of impressionable flesh.

They appraise each other's lovers
with a pornographic eye, concealing in their battledress
the unacceptable reality:

desire, delight, indifference, decay.
Leave the stretcher on the grass,
stand back and let the bugger breathe.

Not long now and he won't be worth the bother.
Somebody dispose of the remains. A floating corpse
can cross a frontier unidentified.

The Thaw

You hear the cracking of the ice,
that clean expression, lifelike,
as the season refuses to pass
unacknowledged.
Already paint is being bought
and lugged in yutes
down to the lakeside:
you have to force the colours into spring
before it does it for itself –
tradition demands.
Smells begin to change
but not in any way you could define,
almost beyond the sense of smell.
Yet the dogs have noticed:
with their broader smiles
and more enthusiastic tail-wags
they encourage the community.
Not long now.
Not long.
Not long before the budding and unfolding,
the split and ooze, before the day
the pessimists begin
already to sniff the air
and tap the barometer.

Chance Discoveries

Deep in the gully
out of earshot of the road,
cold in the shade of an early sundown,
the bones were located,
many on the surface in the fallen leaves,
some cracked open in the jaws of scavengers,
and all as white as moonlight.
Clothing was found in the hollow of a nearby tree.
The area was cordoned off
and in the morning subjected to a fingertip search.
Nobody spoke but in a whisper.
Even a cough seemed profane.

The rest lie undisturbed,
the others in gullies elsewhere,
unstumbled across, unsuspected.
A dog might snuffle through the leaves
but keep its secret from its master,
that preoccupied moron
who thinks the landscape beautiful.

A Place on the Map

Where the slope levels out, a mile-wide shelf
above the sheltered gulf, and what grows
grows low as if reluctant to cast shade,
it's hard to say from what you see
if one city has been sacked or if the land
has been cleared for another.
Are these ruins or foundations?
Is this history or town planning?
This grid in the grey rubble,
these intersecting streets: are we expected
to imagine a glorious past
or some sleek future made possible
by bright plastics and nanotechnologies?
The rubble itself: concrete or stone?
The terrace where the bride is dancing,
the station where a cheek is offered for a kiss,
the square in which a raucous crowd
responds as crowds do to a rabble-rousing speech...
Past or future, record or projection?
Between the two,
                    why would there need to be a present tense?

Boulders

The boulders
at the roadside
have tumbled here
and will tumble further
in due course.
We who drive through
with grating gears
will never hinder them.
They are silence
compacted
by great pressure,
the kind that wrenches constellations
out of the void.
Even this sharp chip
in the split rubber
suppresses a cry.
The fossil of a cry,
it erupted from a boy
when he landed a fish
on the dry cliff
above us, aeons ago.

Said and Done

So gouty, gnarled, preposterous
an utterance as Mr Smith's
between the fish course and the meat,
apparently addressed to both
the Misses Jones, those winsome twins,

bisecting perfectly the gap
between them, or the satin bulge
beyond, the breeches of the page
who at that very moment hitched
his manhood with a candid hand;

so impolite in tone and yet
in meaning so inscrutable
was what he said that nobody
could think of anything to add
by way of conversational
rejoinder but a wordless gust,
a scented gasp of horseradish.

Not till the ladies left the room,
cigars were lit and port was poured
did the Professor rouse himself
to ask, By any chance did you
mean what I thought you did? I did,
unsympathetic Smith replied.

Rhapsodic Materialism

Another night the Russians filled the hotel
with breakages. They tried to register

past offences, already regretting out loud
the scale of the morning's penance.

But each casual mattress, every bankruptcy
in the rest rooms, provided no closure.

One elderly gentleman in high spirits
asked his assistant to appreciate

the twelve new belongings he had pocketed.
The remainder of the bed linen had gone astray.

Between floors the elevator boy, shucking
his brocade vest, demanded a gratuity.

The authorities decided not to hold
an independent enquiry, more fool them.

The chambermaids lined up beside their buckets
all along the corridors, and the assistants assisted.

Dream of the Future

I dream of warfare, the technicalities of strategy,
the exposure of the slope and cover of the wood, the range
of the lighter cannon and the morale of the cavalry.

I dream of peace treaties: the slightest cause and sub-clause, the long
ill-tempered discussions on how to compensate the losers
for victory while rewarding the victors for the same stroke.

I have signed my name to codicils beyond your wildest dreams.
I dream of the decades of peace, with the currency restored
to its original value, the institution of reforms,

the end of rationing and the emergence of a new
generation who know nothing of their parents' sacrifices:
they keep seeking more freedoms than the freedoms they've been
                                                        given.

Without knowing it, they benefit from our strong economy.
I dream of the future, both better and worse, a world of high
technology and low humanity, where labour is saved

by devices but proliferates as a consequence of
boredom, and where computers do what humans once did better.
I dream of more warfare, and pockets of peace, of rocket ships

and space stations, exhausted planets, new frontiers, Venusian
intellectuals with a cruel streak and no sense of humour.
We shall speak new languages and learn to enjoy new perversions.

Making Myth

Gazing down at the sea,
        gazing down from the olive grove
where they say a girl once hanged herself
        as her lover sailed away, his sails
gorged on a simmering wind, his breeches bloated
        with anticipation,
gazing through the gloss and sparkle,
through the shallows at the basalt bed,
        its green hair wavy in a warm wind,
imagining the shadow of the lover's boat
        passing like a doffed cap,
a salute of admiration, not a sign of deference,

        I looked up,
        without looking up,
still gazing into the shallows, their promise of safety
        disguising their dangers,
still looking down without looking up,
        I looked up
into the bell of her petticoats,
        swaying in that warm wind,
as silent as one who has died,
        up into her savaged virginity,
that empty bell, that silence
no one could intrude on, that silence
which could absorb the least sniffle of upset, silence
        like a hornpipe of drowned sailors,
        their feathers ruffled in a sweaty wind.

Possibilities

He pocketed the letter knife
after opening the letter.
No more than a sentence and a half
sufficed to send him down to the stables
for his car.
          You know the rest. Who doesn't?
His purpose was clear,
even as he stopped for fuel
to take him as far as he needed to go.
          The cashier when they asked her
          said:
          he had a look in his eye,
          know what I mean?

Dispossessed of everything but such a look
and a knife with a tortoiseshell handle
a man can still demand of life
and be granted with a shrug
the most extravagant, unlikely possibilities.
          A mere sentence and a half
          can deliver him his destiny.

A Personal Vergil

He moved slowly
    as if in a trance
through the world, smiling at those
    who took him for a knave,
unimpressed by the bluster
that passes for talent and intellect.
    It pleased him to watch
slow events: the cutting up
    of a rusted ship for scrap,
the erosion of a beach,
a youngster's decline into age.
    Nothing distracted him
    from his own distractions.
Life more than sufficed.
He paid the hereafter no heed.

I have followed him
    at a distance
through the predictable labyrinth,
calling him names
    he ignores.

Beyond Progress

Trade with the east,
a reconciliation with old foes,
deforestation in the region of the lakes
for the building of leisure facilities.

The ways of change are familiar.
We play our part with care,
yet errors cannot be avoided.
The event falls short of the ideal.
We make no excuse for our shortcomings
and in any case
we offset them with our renowned innovations:

our satellites and genetic experiments,
our automated systems and prosthetic body-parts.

It's true we sell arms
to the poorer nations,
but we couldn't do so were there no demand.
We teach our children tolerance
and the importance of personal choice.
They seek their own identity.

Intersection

It takes a while in the middle of nowhere
before you recognise it as somewhere...
    reconcile yourself to life
in the stagnant ox-bow
the mainstream has long left on its own.

There will be days of adventurous moods
when you'll strike out in one direction
    or another, in hiking boots
or even in the old truck, heading for
some other part of nowhere,
    an outer reach, a satellite...

    Being not in the middle
    but slightly off centre
of nowhere, slightly off the point, beside it,
you'll find you've brought it with you after all.
You'll find you're in the middle of somewhere:
    Midan Tahrir, Wenceslas Square,
    and you yourself,
the essential intersection, crowded and alive.

The Vulnerable Bead

Life is like that. You know it is.
A girl drops a yellow bead.
Everyone listens to it
bouncing down the marble stairs,
all the way, step by step,
down to the dark basement.

She will never see it again.
Other treasures will accumulate
by the usual processes
of generosity and luck –
a silver chain from her godmother,
from papa an improving book…

At a certain age
she'll start to lock her bedroom
and lock the special treasures in a box
and keep a diary, also locked
with a key she'll wear on a silver chain.
The record of her first

and most intense
emotional attachments
will be followed by her granddaughter,
but then be lost (or stolen)
by the removal men
between one house and another.

Anomaly

The two retired men
walked everywhere together,
one with a stick, the other helping him
and carrying the basket.
One had been a journalist,
the other many things:
actor, teacher, photographer, salesman.

Both had been soldiers for six years
when they were barely out of school.

That was how they met:
in the boredom between horrors,
swapping books
and sharing a tin of tobacco.

Would you expect
under their plum tree or in the upstairs rooms
no one else has ever seen
to find
when, as they must, they die

some manifesto
or even the faintest clue
explaining this so inconceivable
anomaly:

these two, this one, there?

Displacement

Take off your shoes. Walk across Europe.
Eat nothing on the way.
Drink the water out of puddles
or suck on the blades of ice
in the mud of the road. Sustain yourself
on resignation.
If the opportunity arises, steal
from anyone weaker than yourself.
You can forget morality for the time being.

Leave for another time
the making of excuses
and begging for forgiveness.

Instinct will lead you, every dawn,
towards the setting sun

and you will duly come
to the shelf at the edge of the continent.
Curl your toes around that rim,
stretch out your arms and
make as if to dive.
Somebody will grab you by the arms.
Arguments will be deployed,
persuading you to live,
their premises implausible
and their conclusions
wrong.
Witnesses will speak
of how you smiled and, smiling, went on smiling,
perfectly happy, perfectly reconciled, persuaded
by a lack of rhetoric, a perfect trick.

That Sweet

We're eating messages,
chewing on the gristle of
the hard to say, the sharp-edged bone
of what-I-want-to-tell-you-but-
don't-dare. Munch. Crunch. Lunch.
There's rhyme at least,
if not a lot of reason.
I'm reading a whole new course into
each of your expressions –
we ought to have another wine
for each, perhaps a simple
sorbet too to emphasise
a new direction. Munch!
Crunch! Lunch! Music to my
intestines. And think of this:
with fare like this
there's never any question of
an end to hunger.
I'm famished for another word from you,
another phrase, a joke,
a nothing sweet as, well,
as sweet as the adjective itself.
As sweet as that. That sweet!

Narrative Poem

Might I recommend the stuffed cuckoo-clock, Madam?
Jean Tardieu, *The Underground Lovers* (1952)

Two cats are sitting at either end of a doorstep.
One is big and fat and white, the other thin and tortoiseshell.
They eye each other with detached contempt, askance.
Between them on the step, the bowl of cream.

Across the street, the greedy dog.
Beside the dog, the pretty little girl on the stool
and her pretty little dolly, pigtailed both.
On the balcony above the girl, above the doll, above the dog,
the boy who is going to spit.

Behind the boy, between the open shutters
and the open curtains, in artificial light,
the motherly mother and fatherly father
are discussing you-know-what and you-know-why,
agreeing a strategy of containment –
but never in front of the C-H-I-L-D.

In the kitchen beyond the parents,
those disgusting, narrow-minded, bourgeois progenitors,
their daughter is on the phone to her boyfriend.
She can hardly hear him above their obsessive prattling.

At the end of the line, the phone line
(yes babe, no babe, yes babe, no babe)
and, as it happens, at the end of the tram line too,
the boyfriend is naked on his mother's bed,
regarding his erection in the mirror on the wardrobe door.
The man who pays him on occasional afternoons
is fussily adjusting his focus,
craning forward with polite curiosity.

The tickets in his pocket will take him and his wife
to the Imperial Theatre, that lovely old building,
to hear the Italian going through his repertoire.
And after that they'll try to get into the bistro by the river,
the one where you can sit out on the terrace at this time of year.
She can order whatever she wants, within reason.
He'll even say the names in French, if that'll make her happy.

Many women are having their birthdays today,
and so are many men. Some are at work, others at home,
waiting for the day to take its straightforward course.
What gifts will they receive from whom?

On the roof of the theatre, high in the sky,
where acid rain has eaten into Hapsburg lead,
a gang of roofers are playing teatime football
with an abandoned shoe as ball.
None of them can understand
how it came to be lying there among the chimneys.
(The little god with a stye reaches down…)

Nowhere in the city or its suburbs,
nowhere in the surrounding countryside,
is any man with size nine feet,
whether birthday boy or not,
limping about in only one shoe.
Nowhere here and nowhere else.
Not now, not then, not any time.

Rags, a Dog, Eternal People

This tangle, these shreds. Were they worn in this state or have they
rotted since? They seem, like us, beyond redemption; but who's
to say nobody could use them – to staunch an overflow
or mop a spillage? Be careful not to trip on them:
the stairs are steep and hard, the management are not insured,
and life, in any case, is cheap.
                                             A yellow pool around
the bottom baluster, and the labrador is looking
pleased with himself, stupidly thapping the door post with his tail.
Friend or enemy, the same complacency. You'd still get
a yelp and a lick if you turned up with rape in your pants
or murder up your sleeve. He'd lap your bloody footprints with
                                                                                      love –
which is more than can be said for most of our faithless lovers
and brothers.
                       But here at the turn in the stairs, right here
where the atmosphere is icy and your hair stands on end,
here he bares his yellow teeth. He snarls. What he can detect
are mournful astronauts and existentialists, extinct
but on the move, their faces in their hands, tattered cerements
around their ankles, heading for the attic.
                                                            The locals
have a saying about these things. But we must get going.
No time for cracker-barrel wisdom or philology.

Gogol's Guilt Complex

1

Come with me, I said. The city
was growing and rotting at once,
like life or youth or. Lichen
thrived in the corners where nothing had passed.
Come, I said, it's worth the risk.
If anything is, it is. Come with me.
People act like this, they share
accommodation, bank accounts,
diseases, memories. They do
the things we do, but it was we
who learned from them, the long way.
Experience. The university of life.
Bricks and mortar. Material reality –
so much more reliable
than what a fanciful imagination
might have conjured up unaided.
Let's follow the crowd.
The little we might lose
is probably not worth the keeping.
In any case, everything has its cost.
Whatever we do we must pay for.
So why not throw caution to
the sullen smack of heat
that passes for a wind around here?
Take but my clammy hand in thine
– intrepid interlocutor –
and in the other clutch your luck,
or better still your credit card,
and we shall cram ourselves
into a workable tomorrow.

There's nothing more important than your gun,
except perhaps your nerves.
Look after both and the rest will follow.

Gogol's complex guilt
came into the workshop the other morning,
setting the door bell tinkling
with more than its usual hilarity/stroke/ferocity.
I asked who was there in the shadows,
in the shadows I asked who was there,
and a voice with a voice in it
generated animal noises
for the instruments of a meticulous mouth
to carve into
little words, one
after another
after one.
It said this after this
and then that after that,
elaborately leaving my question unanswered.
I asked what it wanted,
if it wanted anything,
and it said what it wanted was nothing…
but 'suffering',
announcing the word like a cake or a tune.
Of that, I regret, I have little to offer (I said)
but the lie in my lie, like the mote in my eye,
made its mark on the scene.
The puppet I was harbouring,
bare on his haunches in the corner of the shop,
began whimpering for sympathy,
but a growl from my visitor
reasserted the need for order.
The lad fell silent.
My visitor fell silent.
I too fell silent, respecting the occasion.
     How can the sinner atone
     for the sin he never committed,
     the effect he never caused,
     without returning the blame
     to the seat of judgement?
It was when he came closer I saw who he was.

He looked at me, shiftily, not in the eye
but from item to item of furniture:
coffee table, love seat, armoire, tallboy...
I am Google, said Gogol, the giggling fool,
I write what occurs to me
never what happens. Revising as I go,
I dot my teas and cross my eyes.

Scenes from Balzac

1   Any man who saw his feet might
have mistaken him for a girl
in disguise – and all the more so
since, like most men with subtle wits,
he also had a woman's hips.

2   He kissed the book
and the two of them wept,
for both of them were madly in love.

3   I cannot but
mangle the language
if only for a moment
to show how oddly
some women speak it.

4   Lucien was like that:
he'd swerve as soon from
bad to good as good to bad.

5   Dress Antinous
or the Belvedere
Apollo in a
water-carrier's rags…

Would you recognise
him as the sublime
product of a Greek
or Roman chisel?

6   He attached himself
to d'Arthez like
a chronic illness.

7   He'll rot before he ripens.

8   Turning back, the stranger seemed
transfixed by the deep and melancholy
beauty of the poet, his makeshift nosegay
and his elegant clothes. Like a hunter,
weary and frustrated by failure,
he seemed to happen on his quarry.

9   'An atheist!' the priest exclaimed,
linking arms with Lucien in motherly idolatry.

Siren Coast
The ship to which the deafened sailors tied
Odysseus made its landfall on the tide.

Scylla, Charybdis
The pilot picked his way between the buoys
And shoals of exhibitionistic boys.

Romance
If you must seize the day, the day you seize
Should have a pirate ship and stormy seas.

Education of the Elite
A euro in the slot affords a peek
Of the abyss from the prosaic peak.

Exploration
The merest infant, first let out to roam,
Disproves the point that all roads lead to Rome.

Taking Turns
The schoolboy actor, waiting for his cue,
Looks like a housewife in the butcher's queue.

Courage
The grenadier was never half as bold
As when he faced the ball the bully bowled.

Epic Poet
Left to himself, unsociable, he whiled
Away his boyhood, civilised but wild.

Productive Resentment
A punished boy believes his master's cane
Has scored his backside with the mark of Cain.

Discipline
The patriarch should hesitate to cede
The least indulgence to his upstart seed.

Traditional Education
Those were the days, when schoolboys learned by rote
The pornographic lines John Wilmot wrote.

Exhibition
The hole through which the old spectator pried
Displayed the role the boy performed with pride.

Superfluity
The monkey's most inconsequential feat
Is that of masturbating with his feet.

After Plato
The one in us is said to hanker to
Become the equal fraction of a two.

Sympathetic Magic
Young couples gravitate towards the fold
In which the farmer's barren mare has foaled.

Figure of More than Speech
Synecdoche: a fetish, part for whole,
Reducing you to nothing but your hole.

Object of Veneration
The most amenable and constant idol
Incites reflectiveness by standing idle.

Over the Top
From far behind, the gallant warlord led
His troops into a thunderstorm of lead.

Post-Traumatic Stress
The shell-shocked soldier, home from war (once bitten
Twice shy) can't stand the booming of the bittern.

Defensive Power
The ancient Britons turned out, when they fought,
Less able than the legions in the fort.

Precedent
The moment he set armoured foot on terra
Firma, stout Cortez led a war on terror.

Less Haste
Unless you're really short of time, do not
Adopt the model of the Gordian knot.

The Olfactory Factor
As anyone who's smelt a fraudster knows,
Integrity's a matter for the nose.

Metamaterialism
How like the rich, to rise above the guilt
They might have harboured for their glitz and gilt.

Appearance Is All
To be a loyal member of the board,
You have to stop yourself from looking bored.

The Mathematics of Redemption
A god who needs ten million people's praise
Hears nothing when the single sinner prays.

No Hope
The optimistic soul hopes to attract
You to her stuffy Heaven with a tract.

Reformation
The Articles that Martin Luther tacked
To the cathedral door were short on tact.

Origin of Species
It took millennia to tell the tale
Of how the human being lost its tail.

Golden Age
Before humanity, an artless world
Was unencumbered in the waltz it whirled.

Material Life
Are humans more deserving of a soul
Than barracuda or the Dover sole?

Life Cycle
The apathetic drunk who takes a leak
Resuscitates a dehydrated leek.

Heavenly
Once he's untied his last flamboyant bow,
He looks more like an angel than a beau.

Infernal
When he removes his furbelows and ruff,
He looks no better than a piece of rough.

To Auden
Of England's greater glories, would you cite
The bleakest and most unrewarding sight
Of slag heaps over some industrial site?

Half Measures
Where grizzlies are concerned, you can't just shoo
Them from your campsite with a well-aimed shoe.

The Contented Artist
When bell-ringers experience untold
Felicity, their bells remain untolled.

Elegist
His lips, half crystalised with rime,
Can't shape a Mayday, let alone a rhyme.

Tradition and the Individual
A shepherd playing on a pipe of reeds
Inspires the poetry a pedant reads.

The Windhover
The poet thrilled to see the falcon soar,
But the supposed ecstasy he saw
Was compromised by pinions old and sore.

Technique Plus Effort
It takes a ballet dancer's ugly feet
To generate the beauty of his feat.

Indigestion
Ungarnished Jonah might put up a wail
To hear the famous echo in the whale.

Trust
A tourist's never more completely guyed
Than by the guy who calls himself his guide.

That Kind of Poet
As flat as sand, with eyes on top, the plaice
Undoubtedly displays a sense of place.

Art for Art
Refined aestheticism frets the censor,
Alarmed as if a smoke-detector's sensor
Had sniffed a whiff of an ambrosial censer.

Mob Rule
In troubled times, mere chance determines which
Is the celebrity and which the witch.

To a Bigot
The virus: you're a better man than I
If you can see it with your naked eye.

Distinction
It isn't immorality that pocks
The features of the victim of the pox.

Dilemma
Which is it more advisable to flee,
The rabid dog or its bubonic flea?

Myth and Reality
Hippocrates himself could never heal
Prometheus' liver or Achilles' heel.

Grave Matters
Humanity, the passenger, from birth,
Is seeking an accommodating berth.

Obsequies
Along the shoreline all the mongrels bark
On getting wind of Death's romantic barque.

Four

An Ordinary Dog

after Kafka

1

The predictable mechanism
continues to function.
The sun comes out, the moon goes in.
Time ratchets up
its old achievements,
a chime on every quarter hour.

In the veering shadow of the steeple,
market stalls
propose a material existence.
Sinew from an angel's wing.
Pearl buttons for a theory.

Greeting their neighbours,
stretching rumour to the limit,
those with better things to do
and others with none
strike echoes from the stones.

Belief conditions them.
The Constitution says how free they are,
the Scriptures how redeemable.

2

Behind the bell an ambulance.
Behind the ambulance a dog.
Behind the dog a ripple of attention.
Run, loyal Argos, run!

To this pageant of cause
and effect, the crowd
adds a collective
speculation.

Yet when the van turns right
towards the hospital,
the dog does not
but scampers on – straight on –

and the bystanders reconcile themselves
to knowing
it was just an ordinary dog.

Theorem

Encouraged to pontificate about the
　　　character of Hensqvist – a
request I've never actually received but
　　　　for which I am prepared –

I would reply, 'He turned his chair to face the
　　　window.' Nobody has asked
me now, but now I shall reply, 'Hensqvist turned
　　　his chair to face the

window.' Without fail, whenever shown into
　　　an English drawing room, he
would avoid the thick of conversation, in
　　　front of the fire or beside

the piano, but would withdraw, with a few
　　　words on an invented
preference for a chilly draught or dislike of
　　　cigar smoke, to a seat in

front of the window. For a few moments he
　　　would follow with his eyes the
conversation that his arrival had barely
　　　interrupted, awaiting

the opportunity to make his move without
　　　giving offence. Then Hensqvist
would turn his chair to face the
window. If, from in front of the fire or beside
　　　the piano, a 'Don't

you agree, Doctor Hensqvist?' came his way,
　　　Doctor Hensqvist would agree.
If a 'Defend me, Doctor Hensqvist' came his
　　　way, he replied, to

a man, that his eloquence was its own
            defence, or, to a woman,
that her beauty was its own defence, thus
            abandoning many

a lost cause for the solace of a view. What
            was it, in views through
windows, that so engrossed him? When Hensqvist turned
            his chair to face the window,

what did he see? When I asked him this, he replied,
            'You,' meaning me. 'Me?
How can you imagine you see me whenever
            you turn your chair to face the

window? Am I to be seen from the window
            of every drawing
room in England?' He began his reply by
            ridding me of the idea

that he turned his chair to face the drawing room
            window in order
to see me. Far from it: my constant presence
            outside windows, he said, put

the fear of God in him; and if he could resist
            turning his chair he
would do so, if only to avoid seeing
            me. 'I turn my chair to face

the window,' he said, 'for two reasons: to see
            the view and to avoid
the conversation.' He paused, as if with the
            intention of allowing

me to imagine what he had meant when he
            said 'You,' meaning me.
My imagination tried to comply. I
            watched him turn his chair to face

a window, outside which a garden arranged
                    with geometrical
precision sloped into informality
        at the edge of a natural

lake. Behind him, around the log fire, his hostess
                    and her other guests
were holding an impromptu symposium
        on heterosexual love.

Beside the lake, in a mossy summer house,
                    sat a man who appeared
to be writing. I was writing about the
        man I could see in the distant

window. As his pause lengthened, I watched him turn
                    his chair to face a
window, outside which the leafless trees of a
        city square could no longer

conceal a wet bench. On the bench, on a
                    newspaper, sat a
man who appeared to be writing. I was writing
        about the man I could see

in the distant window. As his pause began
                    to embarrass me,
and I felt myself starting to blush, I watched
        him turn his chair to face a

window, outside which strollers sunned themselves on
                    a broad promenade,
sleepers simmered in deckchairs on a narrow
        beach, and swimmers frolicked like

deformed seals. In a boat beyond the boldest
                    swimmer sat a man
who appeared to be writing. 'Do you see what
        I mean?' asked Hensqvist, breaking

his silence at last. I saw, behind him in
        the distant window, his
hostess and her other guests, clustered around
        the piano, holding

a symposium on heterosexual
        love. Turning to the window,
'Defend me, Doctor Hensqvist,' said a young man.
        Turning his chair away

from the window, Doctor Hensqvist replied, 'Your
        beauty is its own defence.'
'Yes, Adalbert,' I replied, my blushes fading
        at last, 'I do see

what you mean. I do at last see what you mean.'

Her Hair Is her Religion

for David Shenton and John Griffiths

There is a moment when she looks in the mirror
        and tries not to recognise
herself, hoping to catch her face as others
        see it, whether from the point
of view of a lover as intimate as
        she with it, confirming what
he knows, or from that of a complete stranger,
        trying to see who she is.
She can only be partially successful,
        knowing her own face so well,
but there are times when her 'Christ, you look shitty!'
        comes as if from someone else
and is, as a result, all the more hurtful.
        As if putting a brave face
on that offence, she pouts at herself and narrows
        her eyes, her almond-shaped eyes,
to all appearances ready to conquer
        the offender with one word.
With such abilities as render knowledge
        superfluous and the looks
that make a mockery of moral systems,
        the paradox of her fate
is to be utterly involved in the beauty
        of features not beautiful
at all, or not by conventional measures,
        and although sure of herself
as an icon of taste, hardly less certain
        that she looks like a gnu.
The long-suffering mirror never flinches
        when she subjects it again
to another barrage of squints and curses.
        The more she teases her curls,
the more they tease her in return, reluctant
        to stay put, undisciplined
and intractable, in need of more lacquer

than fire regulations allow.
An armoury of curlers and combs hardly
            makes any headway against
entropy in the matter of her hair-dos.
            That is the way of her world,
a pit of shattered dreams and disappointments,
            or so she always maintains.
But see her on one of her nights, in one of
            her frocks and two of her shoes,
festooned with rhinestones – school of Schiaparelli
            by way of the Oxfam shop –
and you might hardly recognise Her Highness,
            tall as a tree though she is,
let alone her fearless way with a rabble.
            Kissing the air in the vague
direction of each admirer, she flatters
            mundanity with a touch
of her tatterdemalion glamour.
            She has never understood
the old Mirror-Mirror-on-the-Wall syndrome:
            you can't just make midnight eyes
at yourself, fishing for compliments. Beauty
            and love have to be fought for.
She can walk into a room like a rumour
            and leave it like a relief;
but in the end, of course, Destiny fails her,
            like all bra straps and boyfriends.
Suddenly the gentle slope of her slingbacks
            proves precipitous. She falls!
What else can I tell you? She ends up weeping
            bitter tears like cultured pearls:
for perfection is always laddered, just as
            mascara always runs.
The one always runs, the other is laddered –
            and it's not going to stop.

Retribution

When there were trees all over, forests coast to coast, before
the systematic clearance, metal axes, horses hitched
to fallen trunks, the settlement, the farm, the motorway –

it wasn't so important to establish fine distinctions
as we believe it now. A generality would do.
Inventing gods amounted to identifying fears

and giving each of them a suitably unearthly name.
When there were wolves among the trees, and undigested fur
and bones to be examined in their scats, it made good sense

to see the world as an elaborate contraption, primed
for vengeance. Most men carried weapons to protect themselves
from any consequences what they did might set in train.

(A moment of delight – eternity of punishment.)
The population, meagre as it was, had plans to clear
more ground than they had need for, and to build the monuments

their shaggy gods and ancestors were due. Ambitious dreams
of boulevards and landing-strips anticipated what
they couldn't yet find names for, or divine the purpose of.

Testosterone not only did its work between the legs:
it gave men's eyes a visionary glint their dogs and women
already knew was best avoided. Even beardless boys

kept tuning out and staring off into infinity,
already out of reach of feminine endearments and
appeals to reason. Time was ready for philosophy

and sport, with their concomitants the headache and the cramp –
not even such exertions were exempt from consequences.
Although the wolves had been expelled from terraced farms
surrounding

the towns and cities, and although the gods had been conveyed
in stone and relegated to forbidding temples, served
by virgins with fanatical displacement habits, no

one in the streets and market places laboured under the
illusion he was free. Their superstitions saw to that.
Elaborate taboos festooned the simplest daily task.

The body was in bondage, subject to misinformation
disseminated by the sages in the public schools.
An educated woman dared not take a shit without

consulting her astrologer, and dared not visit him
without permission from her husband, let alone her conscience.
Sophisticated times! It wasn't so important to

establish fine distinctions. Which of us is better than
the boy whose first ejaculation made him think himself
accursed? He hanged himself from a forgiving apple tree.

Down to Earth

Could I, dear master, ask a pressing question?

What if there were gods who yearned for us
and needed us to favour them as much
as we, who like to think we feel the dint
of their cool fingers in our mortal clay,
rely on naming them beneath our breath
whenever things go wrong or dreams come true?
What if when we knelt to pray the gods'
uncertain spirits lifted and they felt
a blessing sprinkled on their brows as if
paternally by who created them?

Could human vanity survive itself?

Supposing what we thought were ghosts – the cold
patch in the corridor, the ornament
in smithereens beneath the mantelpiece,
at midnight someone gauzy on the lawn –
were not. Not spirits of departed flesh
at all but gods experimenting with
uncertainty, insanity, disease
and other hazards of humanity
before they dared commit their futures to
polluted oxygen and market forces.

Who could endure a god's humility?

Who could put up with the embarrassment
of having, on the spot, to improvise
an etiquette commensurate with such
upheaval? Gods, for all their condescending
refinement of the form, resemble us.
Imagine having to sit next to one,
unintroduced, at lunch or on the train,
his status imperceptible except
to a perfumier's discrimination,
the faintest pheromone of godliness.

Would you avoid his eye or try to catch it?

They used to say such beings, discontented
with what Olympus offered them by way
of choice, were wont to saunter down to earth
as if into a nightclub to pick up
some unsuspecting specimen of flesh.
Disguise was not beneath them, subterfuge
as natural as knowing everything.
They took it all for granted – what a god
deserved by virtue of his circumstance.
They had the morals of the alley cat.

(What better models for mortality?)

A human you could just ignore or turn
your back on, but a god, disguised or not,
demands attention, even only for
the sake of the attender's self-respect.
As with a film star whom you can't pass by
without obsequiously asking for
her autograph, unreadable across
whatever scrap of paper comes to hand,
so does the evidence of the divine,
off-handedly discarded, leave its mark.

Could you respond without a gormless grin?

Before the brothers flew at Kitty Hawk,
they must have thought of birds and angels, winged
and light, as avatars of liberty.
They must have hoped their rickety contraption
could make a man immune to gravity
and even, therefore, to the wormy sod.
When blameless men have thought of their reward,
they've tended to invoke the image of
ascension – as if all it took to be
divine were feathers and a head for heights.

Is ornithology theology?

The choice is ours, doves or humanity –
and not some simulacrum in the sky
but mortal entities that sweat and shit,
make asses of themselves in love and hatred,
half-heartedly believe in airy gods,
and, knowing we all die, go on to do so.
The meantime is the gist, when flesh is warm
and the imagination fallible
but fun. The skinhead is removing his
torn underwear and grinning up at me.

How could I watch him change in changelessness?

Extinguishing

Why can't I be a little boy again? I'd do everything differently from the beginning
Václav Havel, *The Memorandum* (1965)

Nursing the red fire extinguisher
and careful not to wake it,
he backs across the room and out the door.
One hand on the railing prevents his falling
backwards down the stairs –
it never does to seem unduly
unconcerned about brute gravity.
The world steps back from him
as if unnerved by his untidiness
and the intensity of that demeanour,
drill-bit eyes beneath a clove-hitch frown.
Children and small dogs are called away,
come along now, hurry, come away,
beware that nozzle's unpredictable
array of wisecracks!
His ruddy burden threatening to burst,
he picks the pace up, reversing still
and still the very picture of – well –
psychopathic fatherhood.
Avoid his tongue, avoid his eye,
and give a miss to his vindictive generosity.
Do not accept the slightest gesture,
let alone a gift, from hands like his.
Don't let that careful manicure deceive you.
It's only when he gets outside
and feels his buttocks press against
the door of a nondescript car,
only then does he turn round.
The world revolves around him
till the building stands behind him,
combustible, already lit.
A ragged flock of starlings scatters from
the eaves, all chattering,
chattering their indignation and relief.

Inside the car the valiant fire extinguisher,
no longer constrained
by keeping up appearances, begins
releasing its emotions and its foam.
In a matter of moments
it fills the car, extinguishing the man,
a gush of relief, a rush of it,
a blush of the stuff, extinguishing,
extinguishing, extinguishing.

1   Where will suffering lead me?
To nothing – but I'll have suffered.
Where will pleasure lead me?
To nothing – but I'll have had pleasure.
It's a no-brainer.

2   To hate luxury is not an intelligent hatred:
for it would involve hatred of the arts.

3   Men had touched him
only to bruise him.
Every encounter
had been a body blow.

4   Such trousers! Such energy!

5   A wrinkle of melancholy
which seemed like incipient irony
lined her right cheek.

6   To make of the human conscience,
if only of a single man, a poem,
if only of the lowest of men,
would be to splice together
into one great epic all epics.

7   The dawn after a battle
always breaks on naked bodies.
Who does this? Who spoils the triumph?

8   What they found most interesting
were some incomprehensible pages
about the sins of young boys.

9   Never seeing someone
allows you to attribute to him
every conceivable perfection.

10   There is a curiosity about scandal
      in the secret compartments of bigotry.

11   You can be old,
      you can be prudish,
      you can be pious,
      you can be an *aunt*...
      but it is always a pleasure
      to see a lancer coming into your room.

12   You might have called them brothers
      had they known each other's names.

13   A sewer is a cynic: it tells all.

      The muck's sincerity is a relief,
      and restful to the spirit. When you've spent
      your time on the earth's surface putting up
      with all the affectations of the state,
      the pomp and swank of oath and politics
      and justice; when you've seen the finery
      of incorruptibility they all assume,
      it soothes you to climb down into a sewer
      and to admire the shit befitting it.

14   He progressed with calm anxiety,
      seeing nothing,
      knowing nothing,
      in the grip of Chance,
      or rather, swamped by Providence.

15   I remember once
      in front of the Farnese Hercules
      people gathered in a circle
      to admire him, and to wonder at him,
      so handsome was that boy!

16   No name on the stone.

Empty Quarter

The night is a desert.
As if he'd no eyelids –
    the bedroom no curtains –
    the planet no shadow –
    human life no respite –

mind no inhibition –
body no pyjamas –
    he's tossing and turning,
    exhausted but sleepless,
    through a night of daylight –

the flash of a camera
stretched ad infinitum,
    continuous lightning,
    not a detail hidden,
    not one desire sated.

Each night is a desert
he's resigned to crawling
    across, his provisions
    exhausted and compass
    smashed before he started.

No caravan ever
crosses his path; neither
    does even a mirage
    promise an oasis,
    let alone real footprints

or warm camel droppings.
A beady-eyed vulture,
    perched on its gaunt cactus,
    assesses his future
    and reckons it hopeless.

His eyeballs are grated
by the sand he's weeping,
      but no dose of reason
      could stop him indulging
      this thirsty dejection

as if it were whimsy.
If he begged the silence
      of the dunes for water,
      wreaking a cracked larynx
      on its own dry echo

in the empty brainpan,
could he hope for torrents
      of any refreshment
      but abject self-pity?
      This poisoned well, brimming

with welcome but brackish
and warm, quenches nothing
      but its own attention,
      and that only briefly
      until the next visit.

Rather remain thirsty –
rather starve than poison
      himself with misprision –
      rather live in silence
      than listen to morons –

rather keep his counsel
than be heard by morons –
      rather isolation
      than suffer betrayal.
      He pays close attention

to cold-blooded lizards,
but when they hide under
        small rocks he can't follow
        them into their havens
        of welcoming darkness.

Even if the surface
of his flesh seems scaly
        like theirs, and his hunger
        could stretch in a flicker
        of the tongue to insects

or worse, he grows torpid
with thirst, creeping slowly
        over the dead landscape,
        as flat on his belly
        as they are but further

from its bosom even
than a patient vulture
        soaring on the vectors
        over traffic islands
        or gangs of academics

theorising commitment.
Like all desert dwellers
        he dreams of lush vineyards
        at the time of harvest
        and blue-footed goatboys,

their panting breath heavy
with such potent vapours
        as elicit laughter
        from the very limestone.
        But these disappointing

distractions soon vanish
and he is left dreamless,
        with a dry erection
        and tear ducts as empty
        as a lover's conscience.

His begging for water
continues unanswered.
Such are his unending
nights, seasons of torture,
continents of absence.

He begs for forgiveness
from the empty heavens
or unlikely mercy
from seraphim better
adapted to vengeance,

his voice a grasshopper's
rasp against the forces
of a universal
defeat of compassion.
Such are his nights, nightmares

the imagination
fosters and inhabits.
His hopes are the cornfields
of a buoyant culture
after the last locust

has ravaged and swallowed
the last of its morsels
and crawled away heavy
with over-indulgence.
These nights are a desert

from which he emerges
mortified and blistered,
gagging for cold water
and an even colder
retreat from emotion.

Written After Swimming from There to Here

degenerate modern wretch

Byron

Splish! Splash! Splosh! Wading into the waves,
I whispered my mantra to myself,
don't drown, don't drown, then daringly launched
myself into the depths, lolloping
like a dolphin, but like a dolphin
loaded with lumps of lead. Laughing like
a lunatic, I'd soon swallowed some
of the salty sea and started to
sink. Buoyant as a boulder, bursting
with bubbles, and beyond hailing a
helicopter for help or praying
for implausible powers, I passed
out. Don't drown, don't drown – some dregs of life
lingered, the centre of the senses
somehow spurning surrender, don't drown.
Dragged by a turbulent undertow
of tides, this way and that, passively
propelled wherever the water went,
I waited without forethought for the
favours of fortune. Finny creatures
feathered my feelings, liquidly lip-
synching the directive don't drown, don't
drown, distracting me from the decoy
of death. Let loose from lethargy, I
rallied my resources, rousing these
languid limbs to catch the courage of
the capable currents and soar like
a seal to the surface; but kicked and
cavilled, pettily paddling in
Poseidon's pool. It was destiny
that delivered me from danger, not
the slack and spineless struggle of this
flaccid physique, that shunted my shape
to the shore. I found myself foundered,

bloated on the beach, a bulimic
beluga, still singing my song of
survival, don't drown, don't drown, with a
fresh refrain, succour me, succour me...
Spitting sand with every sibilant,
maddened by midges, as thirsty as
thunder clearing its dry throat over
desert dunes, this clapped out chorister
came to the close of his repertoire,
raddled with regret but not nostalgic.
Needing nothing unnatural now,
neither nurture nor cultural code,
I clung to consciousness, my last lick
at the luscious lollipop of life,
and crawled to my fate in the fierce fire,
randomly repeating riddles and
rain-songs I remembered from summers
spent singing in childhood chapels
and playing penitent pilgrim on my
knees in the nettle patches, praying
for more punishing positions and
dung for my dinner, dirty darling.
I should have sheltered in shade, but lay
lifeless with lassitude, seared by the
sun, fecklessly frowning and freckled,
dreaming of dancing girls, girdled with
grass, and bare-backsided boys bringing
bowls of lovely liquor, laced with love.
But cohorts of caddis flies feasted
their faces on my festering flesh,
succour me, succour me, succour me.

The Lesson of History

1

A stone. A fable. Down among the beehives, brides
forgot their amorous appointments. From the comb
a flight of drones, a flood of honey. Attitudes
of older women: snide remarks and snooty glances,
unpleasant innuendo after Sunday service.
The ploughmen had forgotten how to follow a
straight line. They blamed the vintage, the eclipse, the cost
of living, dearth of single women, global warming
and popery. I ask you! Where a rock delayed
the blade they crossed themselves, but not without the further
precaution of the touching of their testicles
and spitting on the soil. Believable accounts
of pirates. Evidence of rape. Cigars. An eye-
patch, of all things! We watched the breakers breaking. Dusk.

2

The bell for evensong – as good a signal as
a firework or a fanfare that the pub was open.
A fight already, over whose was which of what,
and then a game of darts between the reconciled
antagonists. Above the school the church, above
the church the cemetery. On top of Stillman Point,
the light. Along the ridge, the growing cairn. A lie,
repeated in good faith, and then in less so, finds
its way into the sediment of truth, compressed
by time. The massacre was ordered by the priest,
the king, the trumpet-major. Bodies came to light
like turnips. Dogs became confused, as hungry as
they felt bereaved. Their dribble spattered our galoshes,
reflecting moonlight like so many gobs of sperm.

3

If anyone had heard the news, he kept it to
himself. Discretion was the better part, if not
of cowardice, of obdurate neutrality.
The tongue was an immoral organ, worthy of
the pastor's knife. The children saw this. Rumour fed
a tendency to restlessness in those who had,
and ought to know, their place. A row of cottages.
A pit. A mill. Excruciating hell of childbed.
The scrubbing of the floor on scabby hands and knees,
believing in inferiority and an
eternity of rest. Arcades of chestnut trees,
the scent of their frustrating blossom. Musical
accompanists (the lute, the lyre) at every turn.
A canopy of coral clouds like pretty sunshades.

4

The lamp burned low. Philately and tax returns,
embroidery, darned socks, a game of chess, a snooze.
The bank clerk polished his best brogues with spit and tons
of elbow grease, a habit he picked up before
the army noticed his flat feet. Another day,
another likely story. Fingers used to counting
the money other people spent. Before the war,
the other war, the peace. Political dissent,
the label given to commitment, any kind.
The slightest smile could merit a suspicious look,
an eccentricity a lynching. Parish pump
philosophy surmised a universe without
the litter lout. The weather worsened, then got better.
Embezzlement. Incompetence. A child grew up.

5

Whoever found humanity a disappointment –
as many did who reckoned pubic hair a sign
of moral weakness and the worker's accent proof
of ignorance – was comforted by sleep. A dream
of future possibilities, recurring, lifted
the spirits. Flying trams, metallic clothing, dogs
made out of silicon and carbon fibre, smiles
and spectacles on every face, intelligent
debates about – whatever. Nothing nasty, nothing
unplanned. No scaffolding, no crime, no accidents.
In science lay salvation, but salvation rooted
in common decency, in church and family,
in privilege for elegance, and punishment
for stubbornness. What's wrong with you? What's *wrong* with you?

6

Dawn. Chorus of blackbirds, fighting for status. Pale
beginnings. The first bus negotiated the
interminable hairpins, honking at each one.
Cold, liverish, still drowsy, dopey, people did
what people do. A whiff of wood smoke. Pressure on
the national grid. Penelope was waiting all
this time, preparing breakfast for
that no-good, selfish moron of a man of hers;
then clearing it and laying lunch. She changed her clothes
three times a day – for nothing. Nothing but the structure
of a routine. The boot-room corridor. The bathroom.
Elasticated underwear. A pile of books,
as yet unread. The prospect of another day
was daunting, even to the passionate in love.

7

Confess the worst. Impress the best. Eliminate
uncertainty. Beware of imitations. Try
our newest recipe, with added salt and colours.
The men in uniform will be arriving soon.
Prepare your feather bedding and vaginas to
accommodate their pungent manliness. The port
is under observation. Nobody escapes.
Unless the fugitives are handed over, with
their automatic weapons and their secret maps.
Don't be deceived by these avuncular expressions:
the situation couldn't be more serious.
To disobey would be to put yourselves at risk
of worse than mere detention. Rumour visits the
abandoned quarry near the commandeered hotel.

8

Another gorgeous day of commerce, education,
ambition, hedonism, playground bullying,
religious doubt, erotic complication, envy,
deliberate evasion, usury, mistaken
identity, extortion, laughter, tit for tat,
refusal of the sacraments, recrimination,
hasty alliances, dyspepsia and beer.
Another gloomy night of pewter candlesticks,
those leisurely repentances that occupy
the conscious mind for longer than it takes to lose
your memory, those cramps of the embarrassment
that comes with self-awareness, those imagined ghosts
and realistic nightmares, those beginners in
the wall-of-death of passion, and those sleepy brides.

9

A little circus came to town, a llama on
a length of washing line, a conjuror, a clown.
Erecting their diminutive Big Top, a gang
of stringy striplings, vandalised from head to toe
with amateur tattoos, put on a more enthralling
performance than the one you had to pay to see.
A needy huddle sniffed the air down-wind of their
miasmic armpits. By the time they'd struck the tent
and gone, even the local boys would be with child.
A preacher with a sandwich board is not a match
for hormones, and a teacher with a whippy stick
can be put up with for a thrill. Petition the
authorities. Complain to the police. Apply
to join the golf club. But no Travellers, no Jews.

10

The time of reckoning – as which of any times   ·
is not? Wind turbines on the top of the escarpment,
a dam across the beck. Imagine if we left
the planet to its own mellifluous devices.
The Year of the Bacillus, cockroach paradise!
The undertaker, walking on the beach with his
Jack Russell terriers, discovered the first shoal
of yellow rubber ducks. The conifers above
the cemetery were moulting, needles underfoot
the perfect counterpane for monkey business. Honey
appeared to come in jars, computer discs on trees.
Whoever watched the breakers breaking understood
the simple facts, reluctant though he may have been
to face them. Apathy, with fingers crossed for luck.

Around the Neck

Co-ax, co-ax, co-ax, Brekekekek co-ax!

Around the neck: identity and emblem of belief
on silver chains. Between the lines: I struggle to survive.
The view: a thousand yards of mud. Prognosis: sterile grief.

Ambition: hardly any left but to remain alive,
intact and compos mentis. Occupation: whet the blade
and two-by-four the barrel till the cavalry arrive.

The Book of Common Prayer: of whom then should I be afraid?
Around the clock: alertness to the point of frazzled nerves
and constipation, neither remedied by having prayed.

There's beauty: vapour trails, a sapper's eyes, the light that curves
away from us, the laughter in the voices of the lost
that undermines the protocol of death... He also serves:

who, when the blitz begins, will only keep his fingers crossed
instead of standing to; whose only nation is the ground
beneath his mother's feet; who only fails to pay the cost

of life with sudden death, by luck; who smiled when others frowned
to hear the holy goal expounded by a priest... Ahead,
beyond tomorrow: victory! Prometheus unbound:

escape from tyranny. The value of the blood men shed:
as little as you please. Arrested at the mirror stage:
the Leader, pausing, posing, for effect. His theme: the blood they
bled,

the sacred soil they bled it into, and the righteous rage
their deaths invoked. The land: a nation. All you need to know:
in God we trust, the dollar we adore. Across the page,

another illustration: peasant women in the snow,
identifying corpses. Nightmare: puppets taking flight
across a stormy sky as if they've nowhere else to go

but someone else's tawdry paradise. The sodomite,
the Jew, the black: need not apply. They bring a certain stench:
self-pity, humbug, an obsession with the past. What might

have been: oh, who can tell? Who cares? The gritted teeth, the
                                                        clench
of fists, the cocked revolver: why? The perfect landmine: why?
In truth: humanity could turn its world into a trench

and not regret the landscape. Beneficiaries: the fly,
the cockroach and the astronaut. Ahead, beyond the dawn:
the anti-climax. Questions: did the living have to die,

the dying linger? From High Wycombe to the Golden Horn:
what would a human being not have done to skip the fate
(they ask themselves) of having been conceived in haste and born

to reap the consequence?... Cheer up, my little puddings: wait
and see what gusset-wetting retail opportunities
are being magicked up for you! In any case: the date

has been determined when the poles will melt and tropics freeze;
so seize the day and grab the bargains. Give, for this relief:
much thanks. (These words were brought to you by: *Aristophanes*.)

Butter-and-Eggs

Tenacity, this root
in this fissure,
stem submissive to a salt wind.
            Ignorant
of beauty, innocent of
ignorance.
Given the time it takes
a root to split a mountain
                along the
but against the
grain
like a definitive idea,
after an eternity
        straight to the point –
given the voluptuosity of time,
we too,
accruing wisdom
like the mineral deposit
in each drop of rain,
would take the harder choice
and pit our feebleness
against the rock,
to flourish downwards
        in the darkness, root
and root
into the slightest fault,
we too
into a slab of granite
        glistering
before the cloudburst.

And when the shower has pierced the root
and when the wedge has split the rock
            to open it
        (a grammar at the tenses),
what will have been exposed,
pressed flat and faded, drained
between the pages

but a man

from bone to stone,
procrastination
to an avalanche?

The hand of Aeneas
        veined like a leaf
the hand of Caravaggio
        veined like a leaf
the hand of Darwin
        veined like a leaf —